Series, parallel and series-parallel circuits. Diagrams, calculations, ready-made formulas, explanations.

Series circuit 3

   How to make series circuit? 3

   How to find resistance and voltage in a series circuit? 3

   The units 5

      Voltage (V or mV) 5

      Current (A or mA) 6

      Resistance (Ω or kΩ) 6

      When to use each unit? 6

      Practical examples easy to remember 6

   How to increase voltage in a circuit? 7

      Battery connection tips 8

   How to find R equivalent in a circuit? 8

   How to find voltage drop in a series circuit? 9

   How to calculate current (I) in a series circuit? 12

   How to calculate voltage drop in a series circuit? 13

Parallel circuit 16

   How to do parallel circuits? 16

   How to find R equivalent in a parallel circuit? 17

   How to find total current in a parallel circuit? 19

   How to find voltage in a parallel circuit? 21

   How to calculate voltage (U) in a parallel circuit? 23

   How to calculate current (I) in a parallel circuit? 25

   How to calculate resistance (R) in a parallel circuit? 28

   How to increase the current drawn from batteries by connecting batteries in parallel? 30

Series-parallel circuit 32

   Differences between series, parallel, and series-parallel circuits 32

   Another series-parallel circuit 34

   How to find R equivalent in a series-parallel circuits? 36

   How to calculate current in a series-parallel circuit? 38

Series, parallel and series-parallel circuits. Diagrams, calculations, ready-made formulas, explanations.

How to calculate voltage in a series-parallel circuit? 41

How to measure resistance in a series-parallel circuits? 44

Series, parallel and series-parallel circuits. Diagrams, calculations, ready-made formulas, explanations.

Series circuit

If you line up a bunch of blocks end to end, the total length is just the sum of the lengths of all the blocks. Similarly, the total resistance is just the sum of all resistors.

How to make series circuit?

Building a series circuit is like stringing pearls on a necklace. You start with one, add another, and before you know it, you have a beautiful line of them, each connected to the next. In the world of electronics, instead of pearls, we use components like resistors, LEDs, capacitors or batteries. And here's how you can create your very own series circuit, step by step.

Two resistor in series (diagram)

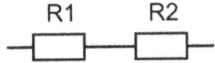

Two resistors in series (circuit)

Three resistor in series (diagram)

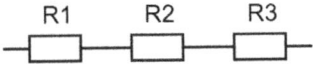

How to find resistance and voltage in a series circuit?

General rule: the resulting resistance (**Rw**) is equal to the sum of the component resistances (**R1, R2, R3, ..., Rn**).

Therefore, for three resistors:

$Rw = R1 + R2 + R3$

Where:

Series, parallel and series-parallel circuits. Diagrams, calculations, ready-made formulas, explanations.

Rw – the resulting resistance [Ω]

R1, R2, R3, ..., Rn – component resistances

For two resistances, the formula will be simplified to:

$$Rw = R1 + R2$$

If

$$R1 = R2 = R3 ...$$

then

$$Rw = n * R1$$

The voltage drop **U** is directly proportional to the product of the current **I** and the resistance **R** of the resistor:

$$U = I * R$$

In a series connection, both resistances and voltage drops across them are summed.

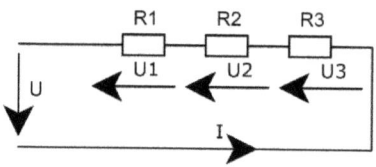

So:

$$U = U1 + U2 + U3$$

Since the same current flows through resistors connected in series, the voltage drops on individual elements are proportional to their resistance:

$$U1:U2:U3 = R1:R2:R3$$

If

$$R1 = R2 = R3 ...$$

then

$$Rw = n * R1$$

and

Series, parallel and series-parallel circuits. Diagrams, calculations, ready-made formulas, explanations.

$$Uw = n * U1$$

If there are only two resistances:

$$\frac{U1}{U2} = \frac{R1}{R2}$$

therefore:

$$U1 = \frac{R1 * U2}{R2}$$

$$U2 = \frac{R2 * U1}{R1}$$

$$R1 = \frac{U1 * U2}{U2}$$

$$R2 = \frac{R1 * U2}{U1}$$

$$Rw = \frac{R1 * U}{U1}$$

$$I = \frac{U1}{R1} = \frac{U2}{R2} = \frac{U}{Rw}$$

where

Rw – the resulting resistance [Ω].

R1, R2, R3, …, Rn – component resistances [Ω].

U – supply voltage [V].

U1, U2, U3, …, Un – voltage drops on components [V].

I – current [A].

The units

Ohm's Law is like the rulebook for electricity flowing through a circuit. It says that the voltage (**U**) across a conductor (or resistor) is equal to the current (**I**) flowing through it times the resistance (**R**) of the conductor. The formula looks like this:

Series, parallel and series-parallel circuits. Diagrams, calculations, ready-made formulas, explanations.

$$U = I * R$$

Voltage (V or mV)

V (Volts) – think of voltage as the push that makes electric charges move. It's like the water pressure in a hose.

mV (millivolts) – when dealing with really small voltages, we use millivolts. 1 mV = 0.001 V. Imagine using a gentle spray instead of a full blast from the hose.

Current (A or mA)

A (Amperes or Amps) – current is the flow of electric charges, like how much water is flowing through the hose.

mA (milliamps) – for smaller currents, we use milliamps. 1 mA = 0.001 A. It's like measuring a trickle of water instead of a full stream.

Resistance (Ω or kΩ)

Ω (Ohms) – resistance is like the kink in the hose that slows down the water flow. It's how much the material resists the electric current.

kΩ (kiloohms) – for large resistances, we use kiloohms. 1 kΩ = 1,000 Ω. It's like having a really tight kink in the hose that greatly slows down the water flow.

When to use each unit?

Use

- **V** – when dealing with everyday electronics like batteries (1.5V, 9V) or power supplies (5V, 12V).
- **mV** – in sensitive electronics where voltages are very low, like in some sensors or audio equipment.
- **A** – for higher currents, such as household appliances (like a toaster might use 10A).
- **mA** – for lower currents, like small LED lights (20mA) or tiny circuits in gadgets.
- **Ω** – for normal resistances in circuits, like a 220Ω resistor in a simple LED circuit.
- **kΩ** – for higher resistances, like 1kΩ or 10kΩ resistors in more complex electronic circuits.

Series, parallel and series-parallel circuits. Diagrams, calculations, ready-made formulas, explanations.

Practical examples easy to remember

- **V** – your phone charger might provide 5V.
- **mV** – the signal from a microphone could be a few mV.
- **A** – a hairdryer might use around 15A.
- **mA** – your smartphone might charge at around 1,000mA (1A).
- **Ω** – a typical resistor in a circuit LED could be about 470Ω.
- **kΩ** – a resistor in an audio circuit might be 10kΩ.

Remembering these examples can help you quickly recall which unit to use in different situations. Ohm's Law is a handy tool, and understanding these units will make working with electronics much easier!

Practical advice. After performing the calculations, check whether, for example, the current flowing through the LED is similar to the current consumed by a hair dryer. If yes – check calculations.

How to increase voltage in a circuit?

To increase the voltage in a circuit, you typically need to add more voltage sources, like batteries, in a specific way.

The key is to connect batteries **in series**. When you connect batteries in series, you line them up end-to-end, so the positive terminal of one battery connects to the negative terminal of the next. This way, their voltages add up.

Two batteries in series (diagram)

```
        BAT1      BAT2
      +||||- +  +||||- 
```

where

(+) is the positive terminal

(-) is the negative terminal

Two batteries in series (circuit)

Three batteries in series (diagram)

Series, parallel and series-parallel circuits. Diagrams, calculations, ready-made formulas, explanations.

```
        BAT1      BAT2      BAT3
      +|||--   +|||--   +|||--
```

Think of it like stacking batteries in a flashlight:

Positive to negative. Place the positive end of one battery against the negative end of the next battery.

Add up voltage. Each battery's voltage adds to the total voltage.

For example:

If you have two 1,5V AA batteries and you connect them in series, the total voltage will be 1,5V + 1,5V = 3V.

If you have three 1,5V batteries, the total voltage will be 1,5V + 1,5V + 1,5V = 4,5V.

Battery connection tips

Check polarity. Always connect the positive terminal of one battery to the negative terminal of the next when connecting in series.

Match types. Use batteries of the same type and voltage for a stable and reliable setup.

Quick recap

- To increase voltage – connect batteries in **series** (positive to negative).
- **Series connection of batteries** – adds up their voltages.
- **Connecting components in series** – shares the same current, not voltage.

Practical advice. Components in series are like holiday lights, where if one bulb goes out, the rest do too because they all share the same current path.

How to find R equivalent in a circuit?

In a series circuit, all the resistors (or other components) are connected one after the other in a single path. The current flows through each resistor one by one.

To find the equivalent resistance in a series circuit, you simply add **up all the resistances**.

Series, parallel and series-parallel circuits. Diagrams, calculations, ready-made formulas, explanations.

$$Rw = R1 + R2 + R3 + ...$$

Here's how to do it step-by-step:

1. **Identify all resistors**. Look at your circuit and list out the resistance values of each resistor. Let's call them R1, R2, R3 etc.

2. **Add them up**. Just add the resistance values together to get the total or equivalent resistance.

Example

Imagine you have three resistors in series with the following resistances:

R1 = 2Ω,

R2 = 3Ω,

R3 = 5 Ω.

To find the equivalent resistance:

$$Rw = R1 + R2 + R3$$

$$Rw = 2Ω + 3Ω + 5Ω$$

$$Rw = 10Ω$$

Key points to remember

- In series circuit resistors are connected end-to-end.
- The same current flows through all resistors in a series circuit.
- Simply add up all the resistance values to find the equivalent resistance.

Quick recap

- Identify the resistors in series.
- Add their resistance values together.

How to find voltage drop in a series circuit?

Voltage drop is the amount of voltage that is „used up" or „dropped" across each resistor in a circuit. In a series circuit, the voltage drop across each resistor depends on its resistance.

Ohm's Law recap

Series, parallel and series-parallel circuits. Diagrams, calculations, ready-made formulas, explanations.

To find the voltage drop, we use Ohm's Law:

$$U = I * R$$

Where:

- **U** is the voltage drop across the resistor.
- **I** is the current flowing through the circuit.
- **R** is the resistance of the resistor.

Steps to find voltage drop in a series circuit

1. Find the total resistance (**Rw**). Add up all the resistances in series.

$$Rw = R1 + R2 + R3 + \ldots$$

2. Find the total current (**I**). Use the total voltage supplied by the source (let's call it U) and the total resistance to find the current using Ohm's Law:

$$I = \frac{U}{Rw}$$

3. Find voltage drop across each resistor. Now, use the current you just calculated and multiply it by each resistor's resistance to find the voltage drop across each resistor:

$$U1 = I * R1$$

$$U2 = I * R2$$

$$U3 = I * R3$$

...

Example

Imagine you have a series circuit with the following:

Total voltage supplied: U = 12V

Three resistors: R1 = 2Ω, R2 = 3Ω, R3 = 5Ω

Step 1. Find total resistance

$$Rw = R1 + R2 + R3$$

$$Rw = 2Ω + 3Ω + 5Ω$$

$$Rw = 10Ω$$

Series, parallel and series-parallel circuits. Diagrams, calculations, ready-made formulas, explanations.

Step 2. Find total current

$$I = \frac{U}{Rw}$$

$$I = \frac{12V}{10\Omega}$$

$$I = 1,2A$$

Step 3. Find voltage drop across each resistor

$$U1 = I * R1$$

$$U1 = 1,2A * 2\Omega$$

$$U1 = 2,4V$$

$$U2 = I * R2$$

$$U2 = 1,2A * 3\Omega$$

$$U2 = 3,6V$$

$$U3 = I * R3$$

$$U3 = 1,2A * 5\Omega$$

$$U3 = 6V$$

So, the voltage drops across the resistors are:

$$U1 = 2,4V$$

$$U2 = 3,6V$$

$$U3 = 6V$$

Practical advice. Once you have calculated all the voltage drops in the series, check that they are equal to the voltage applied to all resistors from the start point to the end point.

Quick recap

Series, parallel and series-parallel circuits. Diagrams, calculations, ready-made formulas, explanations.

- **Add up all resistances** to find the total resistance.
- **Use the total voltage** and total resistance to find the current.
- **Multiply the current** by each resistor's resistance to find the voltage drop.

Remembering these steps will help you easily find the voltage drop in any series circuit.

How to calculate current (I) in a series circuit?

In a series circuit, the current is the same at every point in the circuit. This is because there's only one path for the current to flow.

Steps to calculate current (I) in a series circuit

1. Find the total resistance (**Rw**). Add up all the resistances in the series circuit.
2. Find the total voltage (**U**). Determine the total voltage supplied by the source.
3. Use Ohm's Law. Apply Ohm's Law to calculate the current.

Ohm's Law Recap

Ohm's Law states:

$$I = \frac{U}{R}$$

Where:

I is the current in amperes (A).

U is the voltage in volts (V).

R is the resistance in ohms (Ω).

Step-by-step example

Imagine you have a series circuit with the following components:

A total voltage supply of U= 12V.

Three resistors with resistances: $R1 = 2Ω$, $R2 = 3Ω$, $R3 = 5Ω$.

Series, parallel and series-parallel circuits. Diagrams, calculations, ready-made formulas, explanations.

Step 1: Find the total resistance

Add up all the resistances:

$Rw = R1 + R2 + R3$

$Rw = 2Ω + 3Ω + 5Ω$

$Rw = 10Ω$

Step 2: Find the total voltage

You already have the total voltage: U= 12V.

Step 3: Use Ohm's Law to calculate the current

Now, apply Ohm's Law:

$$I = \frac{U}{Rw}$$

$$I = \frac{12V}{10Ω}$$

$I = 1{,}2A$

So, the current flowing through the series circuit is 1.2 amperes (A).

Quick recap

- Add up all the resistances to get **the total resistance**.
- Identify **the total voltage** supplied by the source.
- **Use Ohm's Law**. Divide the total voltage by the total resistance to find the current.

Easy to Remember

- **Total resistance.** Add all resistors.
- **Total voltage.** Look at your power source.
- **Ohm's Law:**

$$I = \frac{U}{R}$$

This simple formula and method will help you calculate the current in any series circuit.

Series, parallel and series-parallel circuits. Diagrams, calculations, ready-made formulas, explanations.

How to calculate voltage drop in a series circuit?

Voltage drop is the amount of voltage that is „used up" across each resistor in a circuit. In a series circuit, the voltage drop depends on the resistance of each component.

Steps to calculate voltage drop in a series circuit

1. Find the total resistance (**Rw**). Add up all the resistances in the series circuit.
2. Find the total current (**I**). Use the total voltage supplied and the total resistance to find the current.
3. Calculate the voltage drop across each resistor. Use Ohm's Law for each resistor to find the voltage drop.

Ohm's Law Recap

Ohm's Law is:

$$U = I * R$$

Where:

    U is the voltage drop.

    I is the current.

    R is the resistance.

Step-by-step example

Imagine you have a series circuit with the following components:

Total voltage supply: U = 12V.

Three resistors: R1 = 2Ω, R2 = 3 Ω, R3 = 5 Ω.

Step 1: Find the total resistance

Add up all the resistances:

$$Rw = R1 + R2 + R3$$

$$Rw = 2Ω + 3Ω + 5Ω$$

Series, parallel and series-parallel circuits. Diagrams, calculations, ready-made formulas, explanations.

$Rw = 10Ω$

Step 2: Find the total current

Use the total voltage and the total resistance to find the current:

$$I = \frac{U}{Rw}$$

$$I = \frac{12V}{10Ω}$$

$I = 1,2A$

Step 3: Calculate the voltage drop across each resistor

Now, use Ohm's Law for each resistor:

1. For R1:

$U1 = I * R1$

$U1 = 1,2A * 2Ω$

$U1 = 2,4V$

2. For R2:

$U2 = I * R2$

$U2 = 1,2A * 3Ω$

$U2 = 3,6V$

3. For R3:

$U3 = I * R3$

$U3 = 1,2A * 5Ω$

$U3 = 6V$

So, the voltage drops across the resistors are:

$U1 = 2,4V$

$U2 = 3,6V$

$U3 = 6V$

Series, parallel and series-parallel circuits. Diagrams, calculations, ready-made formulas, explanations.

Quick recap

- **Total resistance**. Add up all resistors

$$R_w = R1 + R2 + R3$$

- **Total current**. Use the total voltage and total resistance

$$I = \frac{U}{R_w}$$

- **Voltage drop**. Use Ohm's Law for each resistor

$$U = I * R$$

Easy to remember steps

- **Add resistances**. Get the total resistance.
- **Calculate current**. Use the total voltage and total resistance.
- **Find voltage drops**. Use Ohm's Law for each resistor.

By following these steps, you can easily find the voltage drop across each resistor in a series circuit.

Parallel circuit

If you have multiple lanes on a highway, more lanes mean traffic can flow more easily. Each lane represents a resistor in parallel, and more lanes (resistors) decrease the overall resistance.

How to do parallel circuits?

In a parallel circuit, all the components are connected across the same two points, creating multiple paths for the current to flow. Each component gets the same voltage, but the current can be different in each path.

Two resistor parallel (diagram)

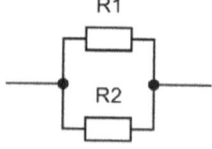

Series, parallel and series-parallel circuits. Diagrams, calculations, ready-made formulas, explanations.

Two resistors parallel (circuit)

Three resistor parallel (diagram)

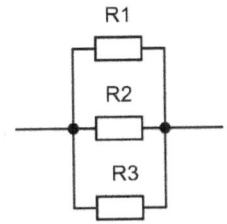

How to find R equivalent in a parallel circuit?

In a parallel circuit, the conductivities (which are the inverses of resistances) add up. Conductivity is how easily current can flow through a resistor.

R equivalent stands for „equivalent resistance." It's a way of simplifying a complex circuit with multiple resistors into a single resistor that has the same overall effect on the circuit.

Steps to find R equivalent in a parallel circuit

- **Find the conductivity of each resistor.** Calculate the reciprocal (inverse) of each resistance.
- **Sum the conductivities.** Add up all the reciprocals.
- **Find the reciprocal of the sum.** Take the reciprocal of the total conductivity to get the equivalent resistance.

Series, parallel and series-parallel circuits. Diagrams, calculations, ready-made formulas, explanations.

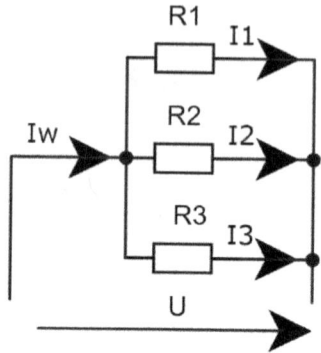

The reciprocal of the resultant resistance is equal to the sum of the reciprocals of the component resistances:

$$\frac{1}{Rw} = \frac{1}{R1} + \frac{1}{R2} + \frac{1}{R3} + \ldots \frac{1}{Rn}$$

$$Gw = G1 + G2 + G3 + \ldots Gn$$

$$Iw = I1 + I2 + I3 + \ldots In$$

If

$$R1 = R2 = R3 \ldots = Rn$$

then

$$Rw = \frac{R1}{n}$$

$$I = \frac{Iw}{n}$$

The ratio of current values

$$I1:I2:I3:\ldots In = \frac{1}{R1}:\frac{1}{R2}:\frac{1}{R3}:\ldots\frac{1}{Rn} = G1:G2:G3:\ldots Gn$$

If only three resistances are connected in parallel, then

$$Rw = \frac{R1 * R2 * R3}{R1 * R2 + R1 * R3 + R2 * R3}$$

Series, parallel and series-parallel circuits. Diagrams, calculations, ready-made formulas, explanations.

If only two resistances are connected in parallel, then

$$Rw = \frac{R1 * R2}{R1 + R2}$$

$$R1 = \frac{R2 * Rw}{R2 - Rw}$$

$$R2 = \frac{R1 * Rw}{R1 - Rw}$$

$$\frac{R1}{R2} = \frac{I2}{I1}$$

$$\frac{Rw}{R1} = \frac{I1}{Iw}$$

$$\frac{Rw}{R2} = \frac{I2}{Iw}$$

$$I1 = \frac{I2 * R2}{R1}$$

$$I2 = \frac{I1 * R2}{R2}$$

$$Iw = \frac{I1 * R1}{Rw}$$

$$R1 = \frac{I2 * R2}{I1}$$

$$R2 = \frac{I1 * R1}{I2}$$

$$Rw = \frac{I1 * R1}{Iw}$$

$$U = I1 * R1 = I2 * R2 = Iw * Rw$$

Rw - resultant resistance [Ω]

R1, R2, R3, ..., Rn – resistances of individual elements [Ω]

Iw - total current [A]

Series, parallel and series-parallel circuits. Diagrams, calculations, ready-made formulas, explanations.

I1, I2, I3, ..., In – currents flowing through individual elements, component currents [A]

G1, G2, G3, ..., Gn – component conductivities [s]

U – voltage [V]

How to find total current in a parallel circuit?

In a parallel circuit, the voltage across each resistor is the same, but the current can be different in each branch. The total current is the sum of the currents through each individual resistor.

Steps to find total current in a parallel circuit

1. **Find the voltage across the circuit (U total).** The voltage is the same across all components in parallel.
2. **Find the individual currents (I1, I2, I3, ...).** Use Ohm's Law to calculate the current through each resistor.
3. **Add up the individual currents.** Sum the currents through all the branches to get the total current.

Ohm's Law recap

Ohm's Law states:

$$I = \frac{U}{R}$$

where:

I is the current.

V is the voltage.

R is the resistance.

Step-by-step example

Imagine you have a parallel circuit with three resistors:

total voltage supply: U = 12V.

three resistors: R1 = 6 Ω, R2 = 3 Ω, R3 = 2 Ω

Step 1: Voltage across the circuit

Series, parallel and series-parallel circuits. Diagrams, calculations, ready-made formulas, explanations.

In a parallel circuit, the voltage across each resistor is the same as the total voltage:

U1 = U2 = U3 = U = 12V

Step 2: Find the individual currents

Use Ohm's Law to calculate the current through each resistor:

1. For R1:

$$I1 = \frac{U}{R1}$$

$$I1 = \frac{12V}{6\Omega}$$

$$I1 = 2A$$

2. For R2:

$$I2 = \frac{U}{R2}$$

$$I2 = \frac{12V}{3\Omega}$$

$$I2 = 4A$$

3. For R3:

$$I3 = \frac{U}{R3}$$

$$I3 = \frac{12V}{2\Omega}$$

$$I3 = 6A$$

Step 3: Add up the individual currents

Now, add up all the individual currents to find the total current:

$$Iw = I1 + I2 + I3$$

$$Iw = 2A + 4A + 6A$$

$$Iw = 12A$$

Series, parallel and series-parallel circuits. Diagrams, calculations, ready-made formulas, explanations.

Quick recap

- **Voltage across each resistor.** Same as the total voltage.
- **Find individual currents.** Use Ohm's Law for each resistor.
- **Sum the currents.** Add the individual currents to get the total current.

Easy to remember steps

- **Same voltage.** Remember that in parallel circuits, all components share the same voltage.
- **Use Ohm's Law.** Calculate the current through each resistor.
- **Add currents.** Sum up the currents through each path to get the total current.

Example to remember

- Three resistors in parallel
- Voltage: 12V across each resistor.
- Resistors: 6Ω, 3Ω, and 2Ω.
- Currents: 2A, 4A, and 6A.
- Total current: 12A.

By following these steps, you can easily find the total current in any parallel circuit.

How to find voltage in a parallel circuit?

In a parallel circuit, all the components are connected across the same two points, so they all share the same voltage. This means that the voltage across each resistor (or any component) in a parallel circuit is the same as the voltage across the power source.

Steps to find voltage in a parallel circuit

- **Identify the voltage source.** Determine the voltage provided by the battery or power supply.
- **Understand that voltage is the same.** Recognize that this voltage is the same across each branch of the parallel circuit.

Example to remember

Let's say you have a parallel circuit with a 12V battery and three resistors.

Step 1: Identify the Voltage Source

Series, parallel and series-parallel circuits. Diagrams, calculations, ready-made formulas, explanations.

The battery provides a voltage of 12V.

Step 2: Understand that voltage is the same across each resistor

In a parallel circuit, each resistor gets the same voltage as the source. So:

Voltage across R1 is 12V.

Voltage across R2 is 12V.

Voltage across R3 is 12V.

Why is this the case?

This happens because each branch of a parallel circuit is connected directly to the voltage source. Imagine each branch as a separate path from the positive to the negative terminal of the battery, all starting and ending at the same points.

Visualizing it

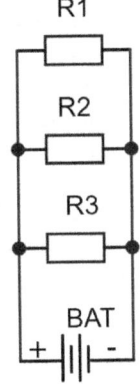

Here, each resistor R1, R2, and R3 is directly connected to the battery's terminals.

Quick recap

- **Voltage source.** Find the voltage of the battery or power supply.
- **Voltage is same across each branch.** In a parallel circuit, each component shares the same voltage as the power source.

Example to remember

- **Battery:** 12V

Series, parallel and series-parallel circuits. Diagrams, calculations, ready-made formulas, explanations.

- **Resistors in parallel**: each gets 12V.

This simplicity makes parallel circuits easy to work with because you don't have to do any complex calculations to find the voltage across each component—it's just the voltage of the source!

How to calculate voltage (U) in a parallel circuit?

In a parallel circuit, the voltage across each branch is the same and is equal to the voltage of the power source. This means that if you know the voltage of the power source, you already know the voltage across each resistor in the parallel circuit.

Steps to calculate voltage in a parallel circuit

- **Identify the voltage of the power source**. This is the voltage provided by the battery or power supply.
- **Understand that each branch gets the same voltage**. The voltage across each resistor or component in the parallel circuit is equal to the voltage of the power source.

Example to remember

Let's say you have a parallel circuit with a 12V battery and three resistors:

Step 1: Identify the voltage of the power source

The battery provides a voltage of 12V.

Step 2: Recognize that voltage is the same across each branch

Each resistor in the parallel circuit will have the same voltage as the power source:

Voltage across R1 is 12V.

Voltage across R2 is 12V.

Voltage across R3is 12V.

Visualizing It

Series, parallel and series-parallel circuits. Diagrams, calculations, ready-made formulas, explanations.

Imagine the circuit like this:

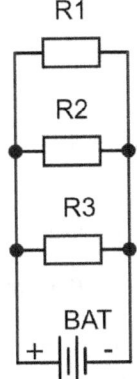

Here, each resistor R1, R2, and R3 is directly connected to the battery's BAT terminals, so each one gets the full 12V from the battery.

Why is this the case?

This happens because in a parallel circuit, each branch is connected directly across the power supply. Each branch forms a complete loop with the power source, so they all get the same voltage.

Quick recap

- **Voltage source**. Find the voltage of the battery or power supply.
- **Voltage is same across each branch**. Each resistor or component in a parallel circuit gets the same voltage as the source.

Example to remember

- **Battery**: 12V
- **Resistors in parallel**: each gets 12V.

So, if you have a parallel circuit with a known voltage source, you already know the voltage across each component in the circuit—it's the same as the source voltage. Simple and easy!

Series, parallel and series-parallel circuits. Diagrams, calculations, ready-made formulas, explanations.

How to calculate current (I) in a parallel circuit?

In a parallel circuit, the total current is the sum of the currents through each branch. Each branch has its own current, which depends on the resistance of that branch and the voltage across it.

Steps to calculate current in a parallel circuit

- **Identify the voltage across the circuit (U).** The voltage is the same across each branch of a parallel circuit.
- **Find the individual currents (I1, I2, I3, ...).** Use Ohm's Law to calculate the current through each resistor.
- **Add up the individual currents.** Sum the currents through all the branches to get the total current.

Ohm's Law recap

Ohm's Law states:

$$I = \frac{U}{R}$$

where:

I is the current.

U is the voltage.

R is the resistance.

Step-by-Step example

Imagine you have a parallel circuit with a 12V battery and three resistors:

R1 = 6 Ω,

R2 = 3 Ω,

R3 = 2 Ω.

Step 1: Identify the voltage across the circuit

The battery provides a voltage of 12V.

Series, parallel and series-parallel circuits. Diagrams, calculations, ready-made formulas, explanations.

Voltage across each resistor U1 = U2 = U3 = 12V.

Step 2: Find the individual currents

Use Ohm's Law to calculate the current through each resistor:

1. For R1:

$$I1 = \frac{U}{R1}$$

$$I1 = \frac{12V}{6\Omega}$$

$$I1 = 2A$$

2. For R2:

$$I2 = \frac{U}{R2}$$

$$I2 = \frac{12V}{3\Omega}$$

$$I2 = 4A$$

3. For R3:

$$I3 = \frac{U}{R3}$$

$$I3 = \frac{12V}{3\Omega}$$

$$I3 = 6A$$

Step 3: Add up the individual currents

Now, add up all the individual currents to find the total current:

$$I = I1 + I2 + I3$$

$$I = 2A + 4A + 6A$$

$$I = 12A$$

Quick recap

Series, parallel and series-parallel circuits. Diagrams, calculations, ready-made formulas, explanations.

- **Voltage across each branch.** Same as the total voltage.
- **Find individual currents.** Use Ohm's Law for each resistor.
- **Sum the currents.** Add the individual currents to get the total current.

Easy to remember steps

- **Same voltage.** In parallel circuits, all components share the same voltage.
- **Use Ohm's law.** Calculate the current through each resistor using

$$I = \frac{U}{R}$$

- **Add currents.** Sum up the currents through each path to get the total

Example to Remember

- Three resistors in parallel.
- Voltage: 12V across each resistor.
- Resistors: 6Ω, 3Ω, and 2Ω.
- Currents: 2A, 4A, and 6A.
- Total current: 12A.

By following these steps, you can easily calculate the total current in any parallel circuit.

How to calculate resistance (R) in a parallel circuit?

In a parallel circuit, the total resistance is always less than the smallest individual resistor. This is because multiple paths allow more current to flow, reducing the overall resistance.

Steps to calculate resistance in a parallel circuit

- **Find the reciprocal of each resistance.** Calculate the reciprocal (inverse) of each individual resistance.
- **Sum the reciprocals.** Add up all the reciprocals.
- **Find the reciprocal of the sum.** Take the reciprocal of the total to get the equivalent resistance.

Series, parallel and series-parallel circuits. Diagrams, calculations, ready-made formulas, explanations.

<u>Formula</u>

The formula for the total (equivalent) resistance Rw in a parallel circuit is:

$$\frac{1}{Rw} = \frac{1}{R1} + \frac{1}{R2} + \frac{1}{R3} + \ldots$$

<u>Step-by-step example</u>

Imagine you have a parallel circuit with three resistors:

R1=6 Ω

R2=3 Ω

R3=2 Ω

Step 1: Find the reciprocal of each resistance

Calculate the reciprocal of each resistance:

$$\frac{1}{R1} = \frac{1}{6\Omega}$$

$$\frac{1}{R2} = \frac{1}{3\Omega}$$

$$\frac{1}{R3} = \frac{1}{2\Omega}$$

Step 2: Sum the reciprocals

Add up the reciprocals:

$$\frac{1}{Rw} = \frac{1}{6\Omega} + \frac{1}{3\Omega} + \frac{1}{2\Omega}$$

To add these fractions, find a common denominator (6 in this case):

$$\frac{1}{Rw} = \frac{1}{6\Omega} + \frac{2}{6\Omega} + \frac{3}{6\Omega}$$

$$\frac{1}{Rw} = \frac{1+2+3}{6\Omega}$$

Series, parallel and series-parallel circuits. Diagrams, calculations, ready-made formulas, explanations.

$$\frac{1}{Rw} = \frac{6}{6\Omega}$$

Step 3: Find the reciprocal of the sum

Take the reciprocal of the total to get the equivalent resistance:

$$\frac{1}{Rw} = \frac{1}{1\Omega}$$

$$Rw = \frac{1}{1}\Omega$$

$$Rw = 1\Omega$$

Quick recap

- **Find reciprocals.** Calculate the reciprocal of each resistance.
- **Sum reciprocals.** Add them up.
- **Reciprocal of the sum.** Take the reciprocal of the total to find the equivalent resistance.

Example to remember

Three resistors in parallel.

R1 = 6Ω

R2 = 3Ω

R3 = 2Ω

Reciprocal sum:

$$\frac{1}{6} + \frac{1}{3} + \frac{1}{2} = 1$$

Total resistance: 1Ω.

By following these steps, you can easily calculate the equivalent resistance in any parallel circuit.

Series, parallel and series-parallel circuits. Diagrams, calculations, ready-made formulas, explanations.

How to increase the current drawn from batteries by connecting batteries in parallel?

When you connect batteries in parallel, you keep the same voltage but increase the total current capacity of the battery pack. This is because each battery can contribute to the total current, providing more power without changing the voltage.

How to connect batteries in parallel?

Same voltage. Make sure the batteries you are connecting in parallel have the same voltage. For example, if you are using AA batteries, they should all be 1.5V.

Positive to positive, negative to negative. Connect all the positive terminals together and all the negative terminals together.

Visual representation

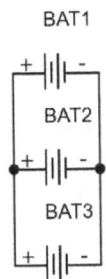

Benefits of parallel connection

- **Same voltage.** The voltage remains the same as one single battery.
- **Increased current capacity.** The total current capacity is the sum of the current capacities of all the batteries.

Example to remember

Imagine you have three 1.5V AA batteries. Each battery can supply 2A of current.

1. Single battery:

   - Voltage: 1.5V

   - Current Capacity: 2A

Series, parallel and series-parallel circuits. Diagrams, calculations, ready-made formulas, explanations.

2. Three batteries in parallel:

  - Voltage: 1.5V (same as one battery)

  - Total Current Capacity: 2A + 2A + 2A = 6A

How to increase current drawn

By connecting batteries in parallel, you increase the total current capacity available to your circuit. This means your circuit can draw more current without overloading the batteries.

Practical tips

- **Check compatibility**. Ensure all batteries have the same voltage and type.
- **Use proper connectors**. Use battery holders or connectors that allow easy parallel connections.
- **Monitor heat**. More current means more heat. Make sure your setup can handle the increased current without overheating.

Quick recap

- **Connect batteries in parallel**. Positive terminals together and negative terminals together.
- **Same voltage, more current**. The voltage stays the same, but the current capacity increases.
- **Sum of currents**. The total current capacity is the sum of the individual batteries' current capacities.

Example to remember

- Single 1.5V AA battery: 2A
- Three 1.5V AA batteries in parallel: 1.5V, 6A (total current capacity)

By following these steps, you can increase the current drawn from batteries by connecting them in parallel.

Series-parallel circuit

A **series-parallel circuit** is a combination of both series and parallel circuits. Some components are connected in series, and some are connected in parallel within the same circuit.

Series, parallel and series-parallel circuits. Diagrams, calculations, ready-made formulas, explanations.

Three resistor in series-parallel (diagram)

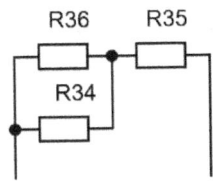

Three resistor in series-parallel (circuit)

Differences between series, parallel, and series-parallel circuits

Series circuit

- **Single path**. All components are connected end-to-end, forming a single path for the current.
- **Same current**. The same current flows through each component.
- **Add resistances**. Total resistance is the sum of all individual resistances.

$$R = R1 + R2 + R3$$

Example – holiday lights where if one bulb goes out, they all go out.

Parallel circuit

- **Multiple paths**. Components are connected across the same two points, creating multiple paths for the current.
- **Same voltage**. Each component gets the same voltage as the power source.
- **Reciprocal resistances**. Total resistance is found using the reciprocal of the sum of the reciprocals of individual resistances.

$$\frac{1}{Rw} = \frac{1}{R1} + \frac{1}{R2} + \frac{1}{R3} + \ldots$$

Series, parallel and series-parallel circuits. Diagrams, calculations, ready-made formulas, explanations.

Example – household wiring where each appliance gets the same voltage.

Series-Parallel circuit

- **Combination of both.** Some components are in series, and some are in parallel.
- **Mixed characteristics.** Parts of the circuit behave like series circuits, and parts behave like parallel circuits.
- **Calculate separately.** To find total resistance, current, or voltage, you need to calculate the series and parallel parts separately and then combine them.

Example – a complex circuit in electronics where certain parts need to share the same current (series) and other parts need the same voltage (parallel).

Example to visualize

Imagine a circuit where:

- resistors R1 and R2 are in series. These two form a single path.
- Resistor R3 is in parallel with the combination of R1 and R2.

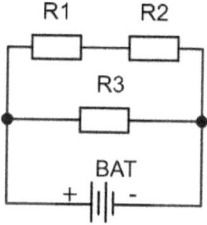

How to analyze a series-parallel circuit

- **Identify series and parallel parts.** Look at the circuit and identify which components are in series and which are in parallel.
- **Calculate series parts.** Add the resistances of series components.

$$Rseries = R1 + R2$$

- **Calculate parallel parts.** Use the reciprocal formula for parallel components.

$$\frac{1}{Rparallel} = \frac{1}{Rseries} + \frac{1}{R3}$$

Series, parallel and series-parallel circuits. Diagrams, calculations, ready-made formulas, explanations.

- **Combine results.** Combine the results to find the total resistance.

Quick recap

- **Series circuit.** Single path, same current, total resistance is the sum.
- **Parallel circuit.** Multiple paths, same voltage, total resistance is the reciprocal sum.
- **Series-parallel circuit.** Combination of both, analyze series and parallel parts separately, then combine.

Another series-parallel circuit

Let's look at the series-parallel connection as a voltage divider

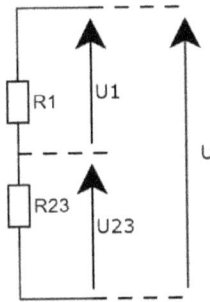

So

$U = U1 + U23$

$U1 = U - U23$

$U23 = U - U1$

Resistor R23 may consist of resistors R2 and R3 connected in parallel:

Series, parallel and series-parallel circuits. Diagrams, calculations, ready-made formulas, explanations.

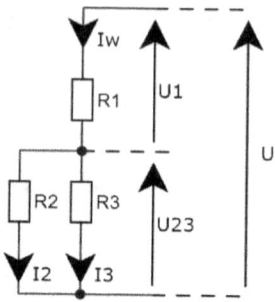

So

$$R23 = \frac{R2 * R3}{R2 + R3}$$

$$Rw = R23 + R1$$

$$R23 = Rw - R1$$

$$R1 = Rw - R23$$

$$\frac{U}{U2} = \frac{Rw}{R23}$$

$$\frac{U}{U1} = \frac{Rw}{R1}$$

$$\frac{U2}{U1} = \frac{R23}{R1}$$

$$U = \frac{U2 * Rw}{R23} = \frac{U1 * Rw}{R1} = Iw * Rw$$

$$U2 = \frac{U * R23}{Rw} = \frac{U1 * R23}{R1} = Iw * R23 = I2 * R2 = I3 * R3$$

$$U1 = \frac{U * R1}{Rw} = \frac{U2 * R1}{R23} = Iw * R1$$

$$Iw = \frac{U}{Rw} = \frac{U1}{R1} = \frac{U2}{R23}$$

$$I2 = \frac{U2}{R2}$$

Series, parallel and series-parallel circuits. Diagrams, calculations, ready-made formulas, explanations.

$$I3 = \frac{U2}{R3}$$

Where

U – total voltage [V]

Iw – total current [A]

R1, R2 – voltage divider resistances [Ω]

R3 – resistance loading the voltage divider [Ω]

R2R3 – equivalent resistance of R2 and R3 connected in parallel [Ω]

Rw – resultant resistance [Ω]

U1 – voltage drop on R1 [V]

U2 – voltage drop on R2 [V]

I1 – current flowing through R1 [A]

I2 – current flowing through R2 [A]

I3 – current flowing through the load [A]

How to find R equivalent in a series-parallel circuits?

A series-parallel circuit combines elements of both series and parallel circuits. Some resistors are connected in series, and some are connected in parallel. To find the equivalent resistance, you need to simplify the circuit step-by-step.

Steps to find R equivalent in a series-parallel circuit

- **Identify series and parallel parts.** Break down the circuit into sections that are purely series or purely parallel.
- **Simplify parallel sections first.** Calculate the equivalent resistance of parallel sections.
- **Combine with series sections.** Add the equivalent resistances of the series sections.

Series, parallel and series-parallel circuits. Diagrams, calculations, ready-made formulas, explanations.

- Repeat if **Necessary**. If there are multiple series and parallel sections, repeat the process until the entire circuit is simplified.

Step-by-step example

Imagine you have a circuit with the following resistors:

R1 and R2 are in series.

This series combination is in parallel with R3.

Visual representation

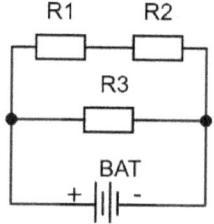

Step 1: Identify series and parallel parts

R1 and R2 are in series.

The combination of R1 and R2 is in parallel with R3.

Step 2: Simplify parallel sections first

Find the equivalent resistance of the series part:

$Rseries = R1 + R2$

For example, if R1 = 4Ω and R2 = 6Ω:

$Rseries = 4Ω + 6Ω = 10Ω$

2. Find the equivalent resistance all resistors:

$$\frac{1}{Rw} = \frac{1}{Rseries} + \frac{1}{R3}$$

If R3 = 5Ω:

$$\frac{1}{Rw} = \frac{1}{10Ω} + \frac{1}{5Ω}$$

Series, parallel and series-parallel circuits. Diagrams, calculations, ready-made formulas, explanations.

$$\frac{1}{Rw} = \frac{1}{10\Omega} + \frac{2}{10\Omega}$$

$$\frac{1}{Rw} = \frac{3}{10\Omega}$$

$$Rw = \frac{10\Omega}{3}$$

$$Rpw \approx 3{,}33\Omega$$

Step 3: Combine with series sections

In this example, you have already combined the series part and found the parallel equivalent resistance. If there were more sections, you would continue combining them.

Quick recap

- **Identify series and parallel parts.** Spot which resistors are in series and which are in parallel.
- **Simplify parallel sections.** Calculate the equivalent resistance for parallel sections.
- **Combine series sections.** Add the equivalent resistances of series sections.
- **Repeat as needed.** Continue the process until the entire circuit is simplified to one equivalent resistance.

Example to remember

Series resistors: R1 = 4Ω, R2 = 6Ω.

Parallel resistor: R3 = 5Ω.

Series equivalent: Rseries = 10Ω.

Parallel equivalent: Rparallel = 3,33Ω.

By following these steps, you can find the equivalent resistance in any series-parallel circuit.

Series, parallel and series-parallel circuits. Diagrams, calculations, ready-made formulas, explanations.

How to calculate current in a series-parallel circuit?

A series-parallel circuit combines elements of both series and parallel circuits. To calculate the current, you'll need to use Ohm's Law and understand how current divides in parallel paths and remains the same in series paths.

Steps to calculate current in a series-parallel circuit

- **Find the equivalent resistance.** Simplify the circuit by finding the equivalent resistance of series and parallel sections.
- **Calculate total current.** Use the total voltage and the equivalent resistance to find the total current supplied by the battery.
- **Determine current in each section.** Break down the circuit again to find the current in each branch using Ohm's Law.

Step-by-step example

Imagine you have a circuit with the following components:

Resistors R1 and R2 are in series.

This series combination is in parallel with R3.

The voltage source (battery) U is 12V.

Visual representation

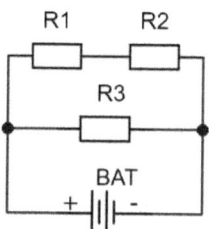

Step 1: Find the equivalent resistance

Calculate the resistance of the series part:

$Rseries = R1 + R2$

For example, if R1 = 4Ω and R2 = 6Ω:

$Rseries = 4Ω + 6Ω = 10Ω$

Series, parallel and series-parallel circuits. Diagrams, calculations, ready-made formulas, explanations.

Calculate the equivalent resistance of the parallel part:

$$\frac{1}{Rw} = \frac{1}{Rseries} + \frac{1}{R3}$$

If R3 = 5Ω:

$$\frac{1}{Rw} = \frac{1}{10Ω} + \frac{1}{5Ω}$$

$$\frac{1}{Rw} = \frac{1}{10Ω} + \frac{2}{10Ω}$$

$$\frac{1}{Rw} = \frac{3}{10Ω}$$

$$Rw = \frac{10Ω}{3}$$

$$Rw \approx 3{,}33Ω$$

Step 2: Calculate total current

Use Ohm's Law with the total voltage and the equivalent resistance:

$$I = \frac{U}{Rw}$$

$$I = \frac{12V}{3{,}33Ω}$$

$$I = 3{,}6A$$

Step 3: Determine current in each section

Voltage across parallel branches:

the voltage across R3 is the same as the source voltage (12V).

Current through R3:

$$I3 = \frac{U}{R3}$$

$$I3 = \frac{12V}{5Ω}$$

Series, parallel and series-parallel circuits. Diagrams, calculations, ready-made formulas, explanations.

$I3 = 2,44A$

Current in series branch (remaining current):

current through the series combination of R1 and R2:

$Iseries = I - I3$

$Iseries = 3,6A - 2,4A$

$Iseries = 1,2A$

Current through R1 and R2:

the current through R1 and R2 is the same as Iseries:

$I1 = I2 = 1,2A$

Quick recap

- **Find equivalent resistance.** Simplify the circuit to find the equivalent resistance.
- **Calculate total current.** Use the total voltage and equivalent resistance.
- **Determine current in each section.** Use Ohm's Law for each resistor or combination of resistors.

Example to remember

Resistors: R1 = 4Ω, R2 = 6Ω, R3 = 5Ω.

Total voltage: 12V.

Series equivalent: Rseries = 10Ω.

Parallel equivalent: Rparallel = 3,33 Ω.

Total current: I ≈ 3,6A.

Current through R3: 2,4A.

Current through R1 and R2: 1,2A each

By following these steps, you can calculate the current in any series-parallel circuit.

Series, parallel and series-parallel circuits. Diagrams, calculations, ready-made formulas, explanations.

How to calculate voltage in a series-parallel circuit?

In a series-parallel circuit, voltage behaves differently in the series and parallel parts of the circuit. In the series parts, the voltage drops across each component add up to the total voltage. In the parallel parts, the voltage across each branch is the same.

Steps to calculate voltage in a series-parallel circuit

- **Identify series and parallel parts.** Break down the circuit into series and parallel sections.
- **Calculate equivalent resistances.** Simplify the circuit by finding the equivalent resistance of series and parallel sections.
- **Find total current.** Use the total voltage and equivalent resistance to find the total current.
- **Calculate voltage drops in series sections.** Use Ohm's Law to find the voltage drop across each resistor in the series sections.
- **Determine voltage in parallel sections.** The voltage is the same across all components in a parallel section.

Step-by-step example

Imagine you have a circuit with the following components:

Resistors R1 and R2 are in series.

This series combination is in parallel with R3.

The voltage source (battery) U is 12V.

Visual representation

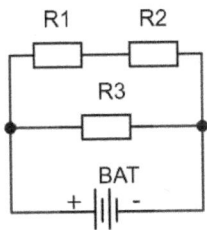

Step 1: Identify series and parallel parts

R1 and R2 are in series.

Series, parallel and series-parallel circuits. Diagrams, calculations, ready-made formulas, explanations.

The combination of R1 and R2 is in parallel with R3.

Step 2: Calculate equivalent resistances

Calculate the resistance of the series part:

$$Rseries = R1 + R2$$

For example, if R1 = 4Ω and R2 = 6Ω:

$$Rseries = 4Ω + 6Ω = 10Ω$$

Calculate the equivalent resistance of the parallel part:

$$\frac{1}{Rw} = \frac{1}{Rseries} + \frac{1}{R3}$$

If R3 = 5Ω:

$$\frac{1}{Rw} = \frac{1}{10Ω} + \frac{1}{5Ω}$$

$$\frac{1}{Rw} = \frac{1}{10Ω} + \frac{2}{10Ω}$$

$$\frac{1}{Rw} = \frac{3}{10Ω}$$

$$Rw = \frac{10Ω}{3}$$

$$Rw \approx 3{,}33Ω$$

Step 3: Find total current

Use Ohm's Law with the total voltage and the equivalent resistance:

$$I = \frac{U}{Rw}$$

$$I = \frac{12V}{3{,}33Ω}$$

$$I = 3{,}6A$$

Step 4: Calculate voltage drops in series section

Series, parallel and series-parallel circuits. Diagrams, calculations, ready-made formulas, explanations.

Voltage across the series combination: the voltage across R1 and R2 together is the same as the total voltage across R3.

Voltage Across R3: since R3 is in parallel, it has the full voltage of the source:

$U3 = 12V$

Current through series part:

$Iseries = I - I3$

Since

$$I3 = \frac{12V}{5\Omega} = 2{,}4A$$

the current through the series part is:

$Iseries = 3{,}6A - 2{,}4A$

$Iseries = 1{,}2A$

Voltage drops across R1 and R2:

$U_{R1} = Iseries * R1 = 1{,}2A * 4\Omega = 4{,}8\ V$

$U_{R2} = Iseries * R2 = 1{,}2A * 6\Omega = 7{,}2\ V$

Quick recap

- **Identify series and parallel parts.** Determine which resistors are in series and which are in parallel.
- **Calculate equivalent resistances.** Simplify the circuit step-by-step.
- **Find total current.** Use the total voltage and equivalent resistance.
- **Voltage in series.** Use Ohm's Law to find voltage drops in series parts.
- **Voltage in parallel.** The voltage is the same across all parallel components.

Example to remember

- **Resistors**: R1 = 4Ω, R2 = 6Ω, R3 = 5Ω.
- **Total voltage**: 12V.
- **Series equivalent**: Rseries = 10Ω.
- **Parallel equivalent**: Rparallel = 3,33Ω.
- **Total current**: I ≈ 3,6A.
- **Voltage across** R3 = 12V.
- **Voltage drops**: U_{R1} = 4,8V, U_{R2} = 7,2V.

Series, parallel and series-parallel circuits. Diagrams, calculations, ready-made formulas, explanations.

By following these steps, you can calculate the voltage in any series-parallel circuit.

How to measure resistance in a series-parallel circuits?

To measure the resistance in a series-parallel circuit, you need to simplify the circuit step-by-step by combining the series and parallel resistances until you get a single equivalent resistance.

Steps to measure resistance

- **Turn off battery or other power source.**
- **Identify series and parallel parts.** Determine which resistors are in series and which are in parallel.
- **Measure equivalent resistance for parallel sections.**
- **Measure resistance each resistor in series sections.**
- **Add resistance series resistor.**
- **Count R3 from equivalent resistance and sum R1+R2.**

Example circuit

Imagine you have a circuit with the following resistors:

Resistors R1 and R2 are in series.

This series combination is in parallel with R3.

Visual representation

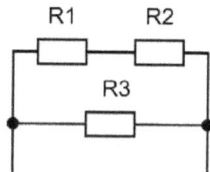

By following these steps, you can measure the equivalent resistance in any series-parallel circuit.

www.ingramcontent.com/pod-product-compliance
Lightning Source LLC
Chambersburg PA
CBHW072054230526
45479CB00010B/1062